Helen Keller

Helen Keller

by Lois Markham

Franklin Watts
New York / Chicago / London / Sydney
A First Book

For Mom, Stephen, and Amy.

Photographs copyright ©: American Foundation for the Blind,
Inc., 2, 8, 10, 13 (left & right), 27, 32 (right & bottom left), 35,
41 (top & bottom), 42, 44 (left & right), 46, 50, 53, 54, 56, 59;
Perkins School for the Blind, 15, 18, 21 (top & bottom), 23, 24,
36; The Bettmann Archive, 26, 60; Grosvenor Collection,
Library of Congress, 28; UPI/Bettmann, 31, 49, 55, 57;
Schlesinger Library, Radcliffe College, 32 (bottom right)

Library of Congress Cataloging-in-Publication Data
Markham, Lois.
Helen Keller / by Lois Markham.
p. cm. — (First books)
Includes bibliographical references (p.   ) and index.
Summary: A biography of Helen Keller, detailing her childhood
struggles with blindness and deafness, and her triumphant life as
a champion of handicapped charities and causes.
ISBN 0-531-20101-X (HC libr. bdg.)
1. Keller, Helen, 1880–1968 — Juvenile literature. 2. Blind-
deaf — United States — Biography — Juvenile literature. I. Title.
II. Series.
HV1624.K4M275
1993
362.4'1'092 — dc20 [B]
92-24942 CIP AC

Contents

Introduction

S it in a dark, quiet room with your eyes closed, a wad of cotton in each ear, and adhesive tape over your mouth. Then imagine that friends and family are in the same room, talking and laughing all around you. You feel their presence, but you cannot see them, hear them, or speak to them. You don't really understand what is going on. You have no way of finding out what people are doing or what they are talking about. How would you feel? Probably you would feel frustrated, sad, and lonely, especially if you knew that you could never remove the cotton from your ears, never open your eyes, never speak.

Such was the life of Helen Keller from the age of nineteen months to seven years. And yet this outstanding woman eventually learned to communicate, not only with her family and friends but with the entire world. With the help of her teacher, Anne Sullivan, and through her own unbeatable spirit, Helen Keller became an author, a world traveler, and a tireless leader of the fight to improve the lives of blind and deaf people all over the world. This book tells the story of her remarkable life.

Helen Keller was born in the cottage on the right,
at Tuscumbia, Alabama.

Chapter One

At Home

Helen Keller came into the world a perfectly healthy baby on June 27, 1880, in the small town of Tuscumbia, Alabama. Her father, Captain Arthur H. Keller, had fought with the Confederate Army during the Civil War twenty years earlier. Her mother, Kate Adams Keller, was the captain's second wife. Helen had two older half-brothers, the sons of her father's first wife.

By all accounts, Helen was a clever baby. Even before her first birthday, she amused family and friends by calling out "How d'ye" to visitors. She also said "tea" and "wah-wah" (water). On her first birthday, she took her first steps. Her early visual memories were of green fields, sky, trees, and the colorful flowers around her home.

This world of vivid sights and sounds did not last. At the age of nineteen months, Helen was stricken with what the doctors called "acute congestion of the stomach and brain." The fever burning in her body was so high that the doctors were convinced she would not live. Then, as suddenly as it had come, the fever went away, and her family rejoiced. Their joy was short-lived. As Helen later

Before the illness that left her blind and deaf,
Helen was a bright and happy baby.

recalled, the light that she could see grew dimmer and dimmer each day. Soon her family realized that she could neither see nor hear. She continued to say, "wah-wah," but without the ability to hear, she could not learn new words. Except for the sense of touch, the little child's isolation was complete.

After she recovered from her illness, young Helen sat in her mother's lap or held tightly to her mother's dress while the woman did chores. Even without sight and hearing, Helen was an energetic and intelligent child. She learned to fold clean clothes and put them away. She understood when her mother wanted her to bring something from another room.

She even learned a basic form of sign language. When she wanted bread and butter, she acted out the motions of cutting bread and spreading butter on it. She showed a desire for ice cream by turning the imaginary crank of an ice-cream maker and giving a little shiver. She referred to her father by putting on glasses and to her mother by twisting her hair into a knot at the back of her head. Sucking on her fingers was Helen's sign for her little sister Mildred. In spite of these creative efforts to communicate, Helen had no idea what words were or how they let people communicate with one another.

Lack of language, however, did not keep her from the companionship of other children. Her best friend was Martha Washington, daughter of the Kellers' cook. The two girls helped Martha's mother in the kitchen, fed the hens and turkeys, or searched the farmyard for the eggs of guinea fowl. One day as they sat cutting out paperdolls, Helen had an urge to cut Martha's hair. She snipped off all of Martha's curls. Martha was about to do the same for Helen, when Helen's mother came upon the scene and put an end to the amateur barber shop.

As Helen grew older, she became increasingly frustrated by her inability to communicate. The sixty or so signs she had developed were not enough for her to learn what she wanted to know or to "say" what she wanted to say. The result was violent temper tantrums. After witnessing one of her tantrums, her uncle concluded that Helen was mentally defective.

Other family members, however, noticed her sweet and loving nature when she was not in the midst of a tantrum. Captain Keller's sister, beloved Aunt Ev, doted on Helen. Once when the child awoke at midnight ready to begin another day, Aunt Ev got up, made breakfast, and started the daily routine.

Helen's mother was also convinced there was nothing wrong with her daughter's brain. She took hope from reading Charles Dickens' *American Notes*. In that book, the English author described his visit with Laura Bridgman, a deaf and blind woman who had been taught to communicate at Boston's Perkins Institution for the Blind. Mrs. Keller's hopes were dashed, however, when she real-

Helen's father, Arthur H. Keller, ran a weekly newspaper until 1885. A staunch Democrat, he was appointed U.S. marshal for northern Alabama when Grover Cleveland was elected president.

Helen's mother, Kate Adams Keller, was a Memphis belle with New England relatives. She was intelligent, witty, and a hard worker.

ized that Laura's teacher, Dr. Samuel Howe, had been dead for some time.

Though the situation seemed hopeless, the Kellers did not give up. When Helen was six, they took her to see an eye doctor in Baltimore, Maryland. He gave the family no hope for her eyes, but he did insist that the little girl could be educated. He urged her parents to take her to see Dr. Alexander Graham Bell, inventor of the telephone, in Washington, D.C. Dr. Bell's mother and wife were both deaf, and he had a lifelong interest in the education of deaf people. Bell advised the Kellers to try to find a teacher for Helen by writing Michael Anagnos, who was the son-in-law of Dr. Howe and was now the director of the Perkins Institution.

Anagnos quickly selected his star pupil at Perkins, Anne Sullivan, as the best teacher for Helen Keller. Soon Anne was on her way to Alabama—and eventually world fame as the woman who released Helen Keller from the prison of her silent, dark world.

Anne Sullivan had come to Perkins Institution at the age of fourteen from the poorhouse in Tewksbury, Massachusetts. She was half-blind. An operation later restored much of her sight, but it took longer to mend her spirit. A proud girl, she was deeply ashamed of her background. She tried to hide it from the others at Perkins with lies and a superior attitude. But two kind teachers were patient with her outbursts, and Anne's attitude eventually changed. She

Anne Sullivan was a young woman of twenty when she traveled more than a thousand miles from Boston to Alabama to become Helen Keller's teacher.

graduated at the head of her class just months before Michael Anagnos received the plea from Helen Keller's parents.

Anne Sullivan arrived at Tuscumbia, Alabama, on March 3, 1887, just four months before Helen's seventh birthday. In later life, Helen celebrated March 3 as her soul's birthday. But on that first day she was far from understanding the importance of Anne Sullivan to her life. In fact, at first Anne was not a welcomed addition to the household at all.

Helen was used to getting her way completely, either through the sympathy of others or through tantrums. At mealtime she ate from any plate she wished, and moved about the room at will. Anne felt deeply for the child and recognized her essentially good nature, but she knew that Helen would have to learn discipline and self-control before she would be ready for book studies.

The first lesson began at breakfast. When Helen reached for food from Anne's plate, Anne removed the child's hand and put it aside. Helen's temper tantrum over this unexpected response was so severe that the rest of the family left the dining room in dismay. Breakfast that day took several hours as Anne insisted that Helen eat with a spoon and fold her napkin at the end of the meal.

When the drama of breakfast was over, Anne introduced Helen to what would become their standard learning activity. She gave Helen a doll made for her by the children at Perkins Institution. Then very quickly, she spelled D-O-L-L into Helen's hand. Always eager to learn, Helen imitated what her teacher had just done, spelling D-O-L-L into Anne's hand. For several days Anne continued to spell words into Helen's hand, and Helen eagerly mimicked her teacher's actions. But it was clear to Anne that Helen made no connection between the object and the word. She still did not have the awareness of language. She did not realize that everything has a name.

The turning point in Helen's education came a few weeks after Anne's arrival. Teacher and pupil were walking outside when they came to the well house where someone was pumping water. Anne placed Helen's hand under the spout. As the water gushed over Helen's hand, Anne spelled W-A-T-E-R into the other hand. As Helen told the story in her autobiography, "I stood still, my whole attention fixed upon the motions of her fingers. Suddenly I felt a misty consciousness as of something forgotten—a thrill of returning thought; and somehow the mystery of language was revealed to me. I knew then that 'w-a-t-e-r' meant that wonderful cool something that was flowing over my hand. That living word awakened my soul, gave it light, hope, joy, set it free!"

There was still much to be done, but the most important lesson of Helen's education had been learned. She

Helen, at about eight years of age, reads a Braille book at Perkins Institution for the Blind.

understood what language was—a way of communicating her thoughts to others, an end to the isolation that had kept her prisoner for five years.

From that moment on, Helen's education proceeded more rapidly that anyone had dared hope. Four months after Teacher (Helen's name for Anne) arrived, Helen knew four hundred words. She could count to thirty. And she could write seven words. Later that summer she learned Braille, a special reading method in which words are made with raised dots that can be felt by fingers.

For more than a year, Anne taught Helen at home. Her methods were radical for the time. Instead of staying indoors and working at a desk, Helen and Anne wandered all over the countryside. Sometimes they had lessons in the low branches of a tree. Anne encouraged Helen's natural curiosity and answered all of her questions by spelling into her hand constantly. As a result, Helen developed a love of knowledge and an independent spirit.

She also became a famous person. Mr. Anagnos wrote about her remarkable achievements in the annual report of Perkins Institution. Soon newspaper reporters were beating a path to Tuscumbia to interview her and Teacher.

Yes, Helen was becoming a knowledgeable and out-going little girl. There seemed to be no limits to where she could go. Her next destination was hundreds of miles away: Boston and Perkins Institution.

Chapter Two

Into the World

In the spring of 1888, Helen, Anne, and Mrs. Keller climbed aboard a train and sped north. First stop was Washington, D.C. There they visited with Dr. Bell, who continued to take a great interest in Helen. She wrote: "Dr. Bell came to see us. He talked very fast with his fingers about lions and tigers and elephants." They also paid a call on President Grover Cleveland, the first of many American presidents Helen was to meet in her lifetime.

In May they arrived at Perkins Institution. Helen had been eager to visit this world-famous school for the blind ever since Anne had told her about it. She immediately made friends with the other children and with the director, Mr. Anagnos, who became a very special person in her life.

That summer was spent at the seashore on Cape Cod. It was Helen's first experience with salt water. Romping in the ocean, she slipped on a rock and went under. When the waves finally carried her back to shore, she asked, "Who put the salt in the water?"

Above: When this picture was taken around 1891, Helen and Michael Anagnos, director of the Perkins Institution for the Blind, had a close relationship. Anagnos was very proud of Helen's accomplishments.

Below: The Perkins Institution for the Blind was already world famous in 1889, when this photograph was taken. Today it is known as the Perkins School for the Blind.

In the fall of 1889 Helen returned to Perkins as a student. One of the teachers had been to Norway. There she had met a deaf and blind woman who was learning to speak. Helen immediately announced that she wanted to learn to talk. Her friends feared that she was doomed to frustration.

In March 1890 she began speech lessons with Miss Sarah Fuller of the Horace Mann School for the Deaf. After six weeks Miss Fuller and Anne Sullivan agreed that Helen could speak. They were, however, the only ones who could understand her. Her speech was thick, and she said everything in one tone of voice. They thought that perhaps they had made a mistake in teaching Helen to form words with her lips before giving her exercises to develop her vocal organs.

Helen had always been sensitive to the needs of others. In 1890, she showed how deep was her concern for other blind children. A minister in Pittsburgh wrote her about a deaf and blind five-year-old named Tommy Stringer. Tommy's father had no money to spend on his schooling. Helen did not rest until she had found a way to raise the money to bring Tommy to Perkins.

A few years later, Helen decided she wanted to help raise money for a new building at Perkins to be used as a kindergarten. With the help of others at the school, she organized a fund-raising tea that brought in $1,135. She was not quite twelve years old at the time.

Helen, age eleven, is seen with three other deaf-blind students at Perkins. The boy is Tommy Stringer. Helen helped raise money to bring Tommy to Perkins.

Helen was fond of dogs. Here she is seen with Lioness. When Lioness was killed, people from all over offered to buy Helen a new dog. She thanked them but asked instead for money to bring the deaf and blind Tommy Stringer to Perkins.

But not all of Helen's childhood experiences were happy and successful. In 1891, for fun she wrote a story called "The Frost King." She sent it to her good friend, Mr. Anagnos. He was so impressed with the story that he had it printed in one of the Perkins annual reports. Anagnos was proud of Helen, and he liked to tell people about her accomplishments. He also thought that hearing how well she was doing made people want to donate money to the school. Before long, however, he regretted his decision to publish her story.

It seems that the story was very similar to a published story called "The Frost Fairies" by Margaret T. Canby. Copying the work of another writer is called plagiarism, and it is considered stealing. Helen did not remember that anyone had ever read "The Frost Fairies" to her. She truly believed that she had made up "The Frost King" herself. But it turned out that the woman Helen had visited on Cape Cod three years earlier had a copy of the story, and she might have spelled it into Helen's hand. Probably Helen had completely forgotten the story. Then, when it popped into her mind three years later, she thought it was an original idea. But some people, who perhaps were jealous of Anne Sullivan's success, believed that she had encouraged Helen to mimic the story and pretend it was her own.

Mr. Anagnos was very embarrassed. He didn't blame Helen, but he gradually became much less friendly to her and especially to Anne. Helen was sad to lose his friendship. She was also embarrassed that she had done something wrong without knowing it. For a long time after the "Frost King" episode, she was nervous about writing.

There was one happy result of this painful time for Helen. One of the most famous men in America wrote a friendly note to her to express his sympathy. Mark Twain, author of *The Prince and the Pauper*, *The Adventures of Tom Sawyer*, and *The Adventures of Huckleberry Finn*, wrote, "As if there was much of anything in any human utterance . . . except plagiarism."

The writer Mark Twain was an enthusiastic fan of Helen Keller. When Helen was accused of plagiarism, Mark Twain wrote her a letter of support.

After Helen and Anne visited Niagara Falls in 1893,
Helen wrote a poem about the experience.

Though Helen had lost the support of Mr. Anagnos, Dr. Bell was still her firm friend. In 1893 he arranged for someone to take Helen and Teacher on a vacation to Niagara Falls. Helen wrote of the water "rushing and plunging with impetuous fury" at her feet.

Helen and Anne visit with Dr. Alexander Graham Bell.
It was Dr. Bell who had suggested that Helen's parents
seek a teacher for her at Perkins.

In that same year Dr. Bell himself took Helen to the World's Fair in Chicago. For three weeks they roamed through the vast exhibits as Dr. Bell spelled descriptions of the wondrous sights into Helen's hand. The officials of the fair gave Helen permission to run her fingers over many of the exhibits. She touched African diamonds, bronze statues from France (her favorite), and rare works of art. The one thing Helen was not interested in touching was an Egyptian mummy.

Dr. Bell believed firmly that deaf people should be taught to speak (rather than use sign language). He urged Helen's parents to send her to the Wright-Humason School in New York City, which specialized in teaching the deaf to talk. So in October 1894, when Helen was fourteen, she and Teacher began a new phase of Helen's education. In addition to regular studies, Helen had speech, lip-reading, and even singing lessons. Teacher believed, however, that Helen's speech was not improved.

At Wright-Humason, Helen and Teacher quickly made a social life for themselves. Helen took part in school plays. Someone tapped her on the shoulder when it was her turn to speak. In winter there were jolly bobsledding outings in Central Park. Helen laughed good-naturedly whenever she spilled out of the sled. Helen even persuaded Dr. Humason and Teacher to let her take horseback-riding lessons.

Because of Helen's fame, she also had a social life beyond the school. She got to know writer Laurence Hutton, who invited her to parties and described her friendly attitude: "She laughed at everything. She smiled with everyone. Everything was pleasant to her. Everybody was good." At one of Hutton's parties, Helen finally met Mark Twain. She put her fingers on his lips, and the great American storyteller told a long tale that kept Helen chuckling throughout.

After two years at Wright-Humason, it was time for Helen to think about preparing for college, which she was determined to attend. Money had always been a problem for the Kellers. In the summer of 1896, Captain Keller died suddenly. Helen was shocked and deeply saddened by his death. In addition, finances became even more of a problem. Finally friends got together a fund to guarantee that Helen and Teacher could live comfortably while Helen was studying.

In the fall of 1896, Helen entered Cambridge School for Young Ladies (near Boston) to prepare for college. Because there were no Braille versions of the textbooks, Anne had to spell every word from the books into Helen's hand. It was exhausting for both of them. At the end of a year, however, Helen had passed French, history, and Latin. She had taken honors in English and German.

The next year she was to study physics, astronomy, geometry, algebra, Latin, English, and Greek. A conflict

Helen reads Anne Sullivan's lips in this photograph taken in 1897.

arose, however, between Teacher and Dr. Gilman, the head of the school. He believed that Helen was overworked and wanted her to take fewer classes. Teacher thought Helen was fine. Eventually, Helen left the school to be tutored privately. In July 1899 she was accepted at Radcliffe Col-

Right: Helen uses a Braille typewriter in her studies at Radcliffe College.

Below left: She reads a Braille book while at Radcliffe.

Below right: Helen graduated cum laude from Radcliffe in 1904 with honors in English letters.

lege of Harvard University. Helen decided, however, to spend one more year studying with her tutor.

In the fall of 1900, Helen entered Radcliffe College. There she spent four very busy and rewarding years. She was far from the typical college student. As at the Cambridge School, Anne had to spell every word of every lecture into Helen's hand as well as many of the college texts, although some books were available in Braille. Helen's chief complaint about college was that she was so busy cramming her head full of learning that there was no time to think.

During her college years, Helen was asked to write her autobiography. It started out as a magazine article but soon turned into a small book about her first twenty years. *The Story of My Life*, published in 1903, was an instant success. At the end of the book Helen described some of her chief pleasures in life at the time. She loved the country and outdoor sports: swimming, canoeing, sailing, riding a tandem bicycle. On rainy days, she liked to knit, crochet, play checkers and chess, and read in that "happy-go-lucky way I love."

Helen graduated from Radcliffe in 1904. She had accomplished the unimaginable. Blind and deaf, she had succeeded at one of the most famous schools in America. Where could she go from there?

Chapter Three

Earning A Living

At the age of twenty-four, Helen Keller was world-famous. There were probably many wealthy people who would have taken care of her for life. But that was not what Helen wanted. She was educated, and she intended to use her education to support herself. But how? As a teacher? A social worker? A writer? She had already had some success as a writer. It seemed logical to try that career.

While working on her autobiography, Helen had help from a young writer and teacher named John Macy. He had spent much time with Helen and Teacher. Before long it was clear to all that he and Anne were in love. Anne, ten years older than John, was inclined to say no to marriage. Her life was devoted to Helen. But Helen insisted, ". . . if you love John and let him go, I shall feel like a hideous accident." That said, John and Anne were married on May 2, 1906. John loved Helen as a dear sister, and he promised that he would take care of her if Anne died before he did. The three happy companions settled down in a large

With the money from her first autobiography, The Story of My Life, *Helen bought a house in Wrentham, Massachusetts. Helen, John Macy, and Anne Sullivan Macy shared this home for several years.*

Helen and Anne always enjoyed being outdoors, especially in trees.
Here they share a treehouse in Wrentham with their dog Phiz.

farmhouse in Wrentham, Massachusetts, bought with the money Helen's book was earning.

Helen was delighted now to have two teachers. She quickly settled into a life of writing with both John and Anne as helpers. Her next book was *The World I Live In*, a collection of essays about how she used the senses of touch, taste, and smell to know the world.

Helen, however, soon tired of writing about herself. She was more interested in the problems of others than her own. After helping to set up the Massachusetts Commission for the Blind, she campaigned both for schools that would teach the blind job skills and for jobs in which those skills could be used.

Before long, Helen found new causes to champion. At the time, many people were concerned about the large gap between the rich and the poor in America. A few wealthy businessmen lived like kings while the workers in their factories and mines and railroads could barely survive. Some thought that the government should pass laws to protect workers against unfair treatment: for example, laws against child labor and long hours and low wages.

Helen began to speak out for some of these causes, including voting rights for women. Many of her friends were disappointed in her political views. They considered them too radical. But everyone continued to love Helen. They said it was impossible not to love her, no matter what unpopular cause she supported.

By 1912 things were not going well for Helen, Anne, and John. Anne had a serious operation. She and John were not getting along well. Prices were rising, and money was hard to come by. Editors were not particularly interested in buying articles from Helen because of her unpopular political beliefs.

In 1909 the wealthy philanthropist Andrew Carnegie had offered Helen a yearly income of $5,000. He gave many such gifts to people whom he felt were doing good for humanity. Out of pride, Helen had refused his offer, but now she reconsidered. Carnegie was delighted and immediately added her to his list of recipients for life.

Helen had been working on making her speech more understandable. With a new speech teacher, she made great progress. She even began to make public speeches about the issues that concerned her. Finally, in 1914, she and Anne decided that the answer to their money problems was to do a lecture tour around the country. At each appearance Anne would speak about her methods in teaching Helen. Then Helen would slowly speak sentences she read from Anne's lips. Finally, when the audience was accustomed to Helen's strange voice, Helen would give a short inspirational message and answer questions from the audience. The public was delighted with both Helen and Anne, but money was still a problem. At times the local managers of the tour failed to pay them after the lecture.

In the fall of 1916, Helen's life was turned upside down. The doctors thought Teacher had tuberculosis. They told her she must go to a hospital in upstate New York for a rest cure. Polly Thomson, a young Scotswoman who had been hired to help Anne in 1914, was to go with her. Helen would go with her mother to Alabama. In the midst of the upheaval, Helen fell in love.

The young man was Peter Fagan, a journalist five years younger than Helen. He had been John Macy's newspaper colleague and had been helping Helen and Anne with paperwork during Anne's illness. One evening when he found Helen alone, he declared his love for her. Helen was overcome with joy. She had never dared hope that a man might love her romantically. The two decided to get married. But Fagan thought it best not to worry Anne with the news nor to tell Helen's mother yet. He and Helen went to Boston City Hall and secretly took out a marriage license.

Before long the newspapers learned about the marriage license. Reporters questioned Mrs. Keller. She was astounded and furious. When she asked Helen if the story was true, Helen, fearful of her mother's anger, denied everything. Still Peter followed her to Alabama, and the two made plans to elope. One day Helen's sister Mildred saw a man on the porch spelling into Helen's hand. Mrs. Keller guessed who it was. One of the men in the family got a shotgun and demanded to know what the young man wanted. Peter declared his love for Helen and said they wanted to marry. But the gun drove him away. The heartbroken young man was never heard from again. And Helen Keller never married.

After this tragedy, there was good news. Anne did not have tuberculosis after all. By 1917 she and Helen and Polly were back together again. (John Macy had walked out on the marriage a few years back, though he and Anne were never divorced.) To save money, they sold the house in Wrentham and moved to a smaller place in Forest Hills, New York. What to do next was the question on their minds.

Their question was answered by Hollywood. The new motion picture industry wanted to make a film about Helen's life. Helen would appear as herself in the scenes of her later life. Helen saw it as a chance to spread her ideas about the disabled. So she happily agreed to make the movie. Soon Helen, Anne, and Polly were on the road again—this time to California.

Making movies wasn't easy. Anne or Polly would spell instructions into Helen's hand. Then she might have to wait up to half an hour under hot lights for the scene to begin. The director would tap on the floor a certain number of times to indicate which action Helen should do next. Though in reality Helen was warm and outgoing, it was hard for her to look natural in such an artificial setting. Her acting, however, was not the real problem with the film. As

Above: Helen, Anne, and Polly Thomson traveled to Hollywood to take part in the filming of Deliverance, *a movie about Helen's life.*

Right: Helen's brother, Phillips Brooks Keller, Helen, and their mother meet in Hollywood in 1918.

Actor Charlie Chaplin befriended Polly, Helen, and Anne during their Hollywood stay.

written, it was a series of scenes from her life. But there was no strong plot, and that is what audiences expected to see in a movie. When it opened in August 1919, *Deliverance* was praised by the critics, but it was a financial failure.

Still, Helen, Anne, and Polly had fun in Hollywood. Douglas Fairbanks and Mary Pickford befriended them. And Charlie Chaplin asked them to dinner. Later he took them to a screening of his latest movie, and the trio laughed and cried all through the film.

When it was time to return to New York, the threesome had to borrow money for train fare. Once more they faced the question of how to solve their financial woes. In the 1890s, Helen's father had suggested that Helen and Anne work up a vaudeville act. Vaudeville was a popular form of entertainment at the time. A vaudeville show consisted of many different types of acts—dancers, singers, trained animals, acrobats, and so on. Everyone had been horrified at Captain Keller's suggestion. It was just not a dignified type of work. But now Helen began to think it might be a good idea. Vaudeville paid better than lecturing, and Helen rather enjoyed the excitement of the entertainment world.

So for two years they toured the country with a vaudeville act. It was much the same as their lecture act except they shared the bill with trained seals, acrobats, and

Left: Helen and Anne appear on stage during their vaudeville tour in 1920.

Above: Helen in a backstage dressing room applies makeup for the act.

tap dancers. During their performances, Anne talked about her teaching methods. Then Helen gave a brief inspirational message and answered questions. Some of Helen's answers were witty; others were profound statements of her feelings.

> **Q:** What is the greatest obstacle to universal peace?
> **A:** The human race.
>
> **Q:** Which is the greatest affliction—deafness, dumbness, blindness?
> **A:** Boneheadedness.
>
> **Q:** Do you desire your sight more than anything else in the world?
> **A:** No! No! I would rather walk with a friend in the dark than walk alone in the light.

The audiences loved them, and Helen was having a great time. But Anne was exhausted and her health was failing again. Toward the end of the second year, Polly had to take her place on the stage. Around the same time, late in 1921, Helen's mother died. Though in many ways Anne had been more like a mother to her, Helen recalled her mother's loving touch in the early years of confusion and pain, and she mourned her deeply.

Helen, Anne, and Polly are seen with their
Great Dane, Hans, around 1925.

Chapter Four

Making A Life

V audeville work dried up in 1922, and the question of money arose again. With Anne's eyes becoming weaker and weaker, Helen decided it was time to return to her real mission in life, improving the lot of the blind. Twenty years earlier she had become a spokeswoman for the blind in Massachusetts. Her efforts had resulted in the creation of the Massachusetts Commission for the Blind. Now she wanted to extend her influence to the nation and the world.

In 1921 the American Foundation for the Blind (AFB) was created with headquarters in New York City. The organization planned a nationwide effort to educate the public about blindness and to raise money for such programs as translating books into Braille, blindness prevention, and the care and education of the deaf-blind.

Soon Helen and Anne began making speaking engagements to raise funds for the AFB. By 1924 they had been put on its payroll. Their goal was to raise $2 million, to be known as the Helen Keller endowment. Helen later wrote: "For three years we covered the country from coast to coast. We addressed 250,000 people at 249 meetings in 123 cities." They raised more than a million dollars, but nowhere near the two million they had expected.

Teacher didn't like fund-raising. Both she and Helen referred to themselves as beggars and housebreakers in the performance of their jobs. In 1927 they withdrew from the work while Helen wrote another autobiography to cover the years since *The Story of My Life. Midstream: My Later Life* was published in 1929. In the same year, Anne had her right eye removed. The next year, Helen, Anne, and Polly went to Europe to give Anne a rest. Back in the United States, they resumed work for the AFB.

In the early 1930s, Helen helped organize an international conference of workers for the blind. There had not been such a conference since 1914. She not only raised money for the conference and welcomed the delegates, she also persuaded President Herbert Hoover and his wife to give a reception for the conference. They were delighted to do so.

It was hard for anyone to resist Helen's winning ways. Back in 1926 she had charmed a smile out of President Calvin Coolidge, nicknamed Silent Cal for his quiet ways. "They say you are cold, but you are not. You are a dear President." Coolidge replied, "You have a wonderful personality and I am glad to meet you." The poet Carl

Helen appears with President and Mrs. Herbert Hoover and delegates to the World Conference on Work for the Blind, which she organized in 1931.

Helen's lifelong zest for living is captured in this photo of her "feeling" a dance at a special rehearsal done for her by Martha Graham and her dancers.

Sandburg sent her a fan letter he had written six years earlier after seeing one of her vaudeville performances. "Possibly the finest thing about your performance is that those who hear and see you feel that zest for living, the zest you radiate, is more important than any formula about how to live life." To the famous scientist Albert Einstein, Helen had said, "You have always inspired me." Einstein had replied, "I have been a great admirer of you always." And when she asked the radio broadcaster Will Rogers to appeal over the air for money to supply talking books to the blind, he telegraphed, "Anything you want OK."

It was Helen's deep need to communicate that made her reach out to people, both famous and unknown. But she was not above using her remarkable friendliness to further the cause of the disabled. In 1929 she had sent a letter to the new governor of New York, Franklin Delano Roosevelt, who was paralyzed and used a wheelchair to get around. When he was elected President in 1932, she sought his aid in helping the blind and convinced him to let the blind run newsstands in government buildings. He later told Will Rogers, "Anything Helen Keller is for, I am for."

As Helen's public work for the blind blossomed and grew ever more successful, however, her private life was heading for tragedy. Anne Sullivan's health continued to fail. In April 1936 she had a final eye operation, but she was all but blind now. On October 20, 1936, Helen's beloved Teacher died.

No one would ever take Anne's place beside Helen. Mark Twain and others had noted that the two made one perfect whole. But Polly Thomson had now been with Helen for twenty-two years. She did her best to provide what Helen needed: the eyes and ears of a constant companion who could keep her informed by spelling constantly into her hand.

To recuperate from the ordeal of Anne's death, Polly and Helen traveled to Scotland. But the world would not leave Helen Keller alone. She soon received an invitation to promote the cause of the blind in Japan. On April 1, 1937, she set sail for Japan. On her arrival she was greeted by thousands of children waving Japanese and American flags. Her tour of thirty-nine Japanese cities was a triumph.

Back from Asia, she again took up her work for the AFB. Earlier she had quarreled with its leaders. They wanted her to spend more time raising funds for talking books for the blind. Helen thought they were neglecting their work with the deaf-blind, the cause dearest to her heart. Eventually though, they smoothed over their differences, and Helen resumed working for the AFB.

Helen had been wanting to write a book about Teacher's life. But without Anne to help her, she found it hard to make herself write. She kept saying she needed more peace and quiet. In 1938 she and Polly sold the house in Forest Hills. The AFB built them a comfortable home in Westport, Connecticut. They hoped it would be a quiet

*Helen and Polly partake of refreshments on their
visit to Japan in 1937.*

Helen and Polly share a quiet moment together in 1948. After Anne Sullivan's death, Polly Thomson became Helen's eyes and ears.

retreat from the demands of the world while Helen tackled the tough job of writing an honest book about the woman who had given her her life. Progress was slow.

When the United States entered World War II in 1941, Helen longed to be of service to her country. She began to visit wounded soldiers, especially those who had been blinded. Eventually she made a cross-country tour of army hospitals. Some soldiers said that just the touch of her hand was a comfort. To Helen, it was "the crowning experience of my life."

After the war, Helen and Polly again took up their world travels. They were in Europe in 1946 to raise money for the American Foundation for the Overseas Blind (AFOB) when they learned that the house in Westport had

Helen campaigned for training and jobs for blind workers. Here she visits the Industrial Home for the Blind in Brooklyn, New York, in 1943.

burned to the ground. All of Helen's work on the biography of Teacher had been destroyed. The house was rebuilt in ten months, but Helen could not face the task of beginning the book again.

In 1948, they toured Australia, New Zealand, and Japan. In the spring of 1950 they were back in Europe. February 1951 saw them in South Africa, where Helen voluntarily held back her criticism of segregation so as not to endanger her work for the blind. In 1952 she and Polly were in the Mideast (Egypt, Lebanon, Syria, Jordan, and Israel). In 1953 they toured Latin America, and in 1955 it was back to Japan and on to India. Their last trip was to Scandinavia in 1957.

Helen visits the Eternal Light at her last home,
Arcan Ridge, in Westport, Connecticut.

In 1952 Helen was invited to Cairo by the Egyptian government to help design a program for Egypt's blind. Here Helen examines an ancient Egyptian monument at the Antiquities Museum in Cairo.

The Soviet Union and China were still on Helen's list of places she wanted to visit. But it was not to be. Polly's health had been failing for years. Each trip had their friends wondering if Polly would return alive. In 1957 she became a complete invalid. Helen's traveling days were over.

As far back as 1954, friends had noticed that Helen herself was beginning to age. Her fingers seemed less sensitive to manual spelling, and she had to warm them before reading Braille. However, her spirits remained joyful. A Connecticut neighbor was enchanted by her "almost girlish excitement and her laughter and her intense interest in everything."

She had finished the book about Teacher in 1954. But sales were disappointing, and some critics commented that Helen's writing was old-fashioned. In 1957 Teacher again became the object of public attention when William Gibson wrote a play about her and Helen for television. *The Miracle Worker* was a great success and later became a popular Broadway drama starring Patty Duke as the young Helen and Anne Bancroft as Teacher.

On March 21, 1960, Polly Thomas died. Helen still had many friends, but the two great companions of her life were both gone. She retreated more and more from the world. Later that year, on her eightieth birthday, she stated, "I will always—as long as I have breath—work for the

Helen meets with actress Patty Duke, who portrayed the young Helen Keller in William Gibson's drama The Miracle Worker.

handicapped." The spirit was still strong, but the body was failing. In October 1961 she had a slight stroke. She lingered another seven years, but she was confined to her home. On June 1, 1968, Helen Keller died.

In her long and full life, Helen Keller had done much to aid the handicapped of the world. But for all of her fund-

raising and education efforts, it may be that the greatest gift she had given was her unquenchable spirit. More than any-one else in the history of the world, Helen Keller had shown that the body did not have to limit the spirit. To her all things were possible. That was her message. And that was her life.

For Further Reading

Gibson, William. *The Miracle Worker*. New York: Knopf, 1957.

Harrity, Richard, and Ralph G. Martin. *The Three Lives of Helen Keller*. Garden City, NY: Doubleday, 1962.

Hunter, Nigel. *Helen Keller*. Bookwright Press, 1986.

Keller, Helen. *Midstream: My Later Life*. Garden City, NY: Doubleday, 1929.

____. *The Story of My Life*. Garden City, NY: Doubleday, 1905.

Lash, Joseph. *Helen and Teacher*. New York: Delacorte, 1980.

Peare, Catherine Owens. *The Helen Keller Story*. New York: T.Y. Crowell, 1959.

Wepman, Dennis. *Helen Keller: Humanitarian*. New York: Chelsea House, 1987.

Index

About the Author

Lois Markham has been a writer and editor for over twenty years. She is the author of biographies of Theodore Roosevelt and Thomas Edison. Most recently, she has contributed to the reference book *World Explorers and Discoverers* and written *The Twentieth Century, Volume 1: The Progressive Era and World War I.* She is a contributor to *Kids Discover* magazine, for which she has written issues on the Senses, Bubbles, and Christopher Columbus.

Ms. Markham lives in Massachusetts with her husband and daughter.